IPHONE
XS MAX
USER MANUAL
FOR **NEWCOMERS**

Complete iOS 12 guide
for beginners and seniors

Stephen W. Rock

Dedicated to all my readers

Acknowledgement

Ii want to say a very big thank you to Michael Lime, a 3D builder, my colleague. He gave me moral support throughout the process of writing this book.

Table of Contents

Introduction

The title of this book already gives a hint on what the book is about. It is a guide for new users of the iPhone XS Max.

There are about eight detailed chapters in the book. Dividing the whole book into three parts, the first part introduces you into how to explore the iPhone XS Max, the middle exposes a comprehensive list of tricks and how to execute them, while the last part culminates with useful maintenance tips, including battery and overall iPhone.

Also, with the comprehensive list of commands, you'll definitely learn to be a pro in using Siri, Apple's voice assistant. You'll be a pro in using Apple Pay. You'll be an iOS 12 pro. Yes, an iOS 12 pro.

Now, start savoring the content of this book.

Chapter 1

The IPhone XS Max

It's the elephant in the room. When this guy was released in September 28, 2018, we were all blown away by the size. With a 6.5 inch display (16.51 cm), it is said to be the biggest in iPhone history. It beats the iPhone X and XS of 5.8 inches.

You might think it's great and I do too. You can now watch videos on a large screen and enjoy full display. But on the other hand, swiping from the very top of the enormous screen with one hand can be very tiring. You finally reach up to the top but then you want to hit back and you have to travel down.

With camera though, no difference. You still get the same 12mp wide (f/1.8) and telephoto (f/2.4) as iPhone XS. But in low light, the new Smart HDR and large sensor helps to reduce grain. It also gives you sweet color accuracy and bokeh.

Now of course with battery, you show expect much more. With a mAh of 3174, it's been tested to last for over 12 hours with normal usage. It's also charges faster because of the tighter coil design

It's also equipped with an A12 Bionic chip like iPhone XS unlike iPhone X A11. Unlike iPhone X iOS 11 too, It operates on iOS 12. It also has Hexa Core with 64 bit architecture and 4GB RAM

The iPhone X Max is wrapped around with glass. Though thick, it's still prone to crash, so it's best you buy a case. Y'know, save your investment while you still can. This bad boy also has a water resistance of IP68 which is better that the previous IP67 as it can stay under water of up to 2 meters (6.6 feet) for about 30 minutes. Now that's a massive improvement from the previous 3 feet.

Its got a storage of 64GB and 256GB. And you can choose to buy the higher storage of 512GB.
As with weight, of course it should be heavier it's not big for nothing. It weighs up to 7.3 ounces lot higher than iPhone X 6.1 and XS 6.2

Chapter 2

How To Secure Your iPhone With Face ID

Setting up Face ID

Before we set anything up, let's make sure there's nothing blocking your face or the phones TrueDepth camera. Try to keep the phone with arms length. And don't worry about contacts or glasses, Face ID can work with them.

To set it up,

1. Go to **Settings**
2. Choose **Face ID and Passcode**. Enter your passcode.
3. Select **Set up Face ID**
4. Put your phone in front of your face and hit **Get started**.
5. Make sure your face is in the frame. Move your head gently to complete the circle. When it's done, hit **Continue**.

6. You'll be asked to do it a second time. Do the same thing and click **Done**.

Using the Face ID

Tap to wake or raise to wake your phone. Hold it in portrait orientation and it should scan your face.
If you're in bright sunlight, you might want to bring the camera closer to your face.

Face ID has been tested to unlock even when you're wearing sunglasses, but not all. So if you're trying to unlock your phone but it isn't recognizing, pull the sunglass off.

How To Charge iPhone Wirelessly.

Later versions of iPhone (iPhone 8 and higher) have a glass back that enables Qi certified chargers to charge the phone wirelessly. There are many Qi certified chargers. But there are two which are Apple certified; Mophie and Belkin.

Charging wirelessly

To charge wirelessly, what you want to do is;
1. Plug your charger to the power. Be sure to use a power adapter that's recommended by the manufacturer.
2. Make sure to put your charger on a flat surface
3. Lay your iPhone in the middle of the charger with its screen facing upwards and your phone should start charging

That not all. Here are a few things to make to wireless charging run smoothly
- If vibration is turned on, your phone might very well move its position when it gets a notification as you're charging. Try to turn off vibration, at least when you charge
- Make sure your phone isn't connected to a USB when you're charging wirelessly, it won't charge.

- If your iPhone has a thick or magnetic case, remove it before charging. It might charge slowly or not at all.
- When charging, your phone might get somewhat hot. When it does, move it to a cooler environment.

Chapter 3

Tips And Tricks For iPhone XS Max

Start using Siri

On your iPhone XS Max, you have two ways to access Siri. Siri is Apple's virtual assistant and can be quite helpful. It can help you perform certain tasks or answer some questions you ask it.

One way to launch Siri is to
1. Go to **Settings**
2. Choose **Siri & Search**
3. Select '**Listen For 'Hey Siri**'. Obey the instructions it tells you to do
4. From now, you can call Siri by saying "Hey Siri"

Another way is to press and hold the button at the side of the phone. Once you do this, Siri should show up.

Learn the Gestures

I'm sure you were a little taken aback when you saw that the iPhone XS Max comes without a home button. Believe me we were not expecting that. But apple has replaced that with features that I think are way cooler. And it only gets better with the fact that they are way too easy to navigate.

One of them is the swiping from the bottom of the display to gain access to the home screen. Another is swiping to the bottom of the screen to open the control center.

If you want to open recently used apps, just swipe up and make sure to hold for some time.

Extra muscle to Augmented Reality.

In your iPhone XS Max, you should see a measure app. This app is available to iOS 12 devices. What it does is, it uses your phones AR (Augmented Reality) potentials to give you a nice experience.

To make use of this, Open up the app. You should see a plus button, press it and use it to make different points in the three dimensional surface. You can use this to measure full rectangles or single lines. To copy it, tap on a figure.

To take a photo of your measurements, use the shutter button.

Use Face ID

The home button is gone, but Apple has provided a sweet way to unlock our iPhones. It's called **Face ID**. What Face ID does is that it saves the information on your face and uses it to unlock your phone next time you show it.

You've got to set it up before you can use it. First make sure that you are in a place with good lighting. Then;

1. Go to **Settings**
2. Select **Face ID and Passcode**. If you don't have a Passcode, you'll be asked to create one.
3. Choose **Setup Face ID**
4. Next you'll have to scan your face two times. Follow the instructions it gives.
5. Now, when your phone is in lock screen, swipe up and put the phone to your face.

Taking screenshots

For those coming from old iPhones or Android, taking a screenshot on the iPhone XS Max can be a little confusing. Y'know, with the homescreen gone and all.

But it's fairly easy. Just hold down the volume up button and the power button together. After you do this, your phone will shine white and you should see a small screenshot thumbnail at the bottom corner of the screen. After taking screenshot, you can even edit it so as to crop out unwanted places.

Setting up apple pay

With your iPhone XS Max, apple makes life much easier with **Apple Pay**. With it, you can pay for items easily without bringing your wallet; all you need is your iPhone. To use Apple Pay, you've got to add your card to the wallet

1. Enter **Settings**
2. Choose **Wallet and Apple pay**
3. Select **Apple Pay**

It's really simple to use Apple Pay after it is set. Hit the lock button quickly at the right side of the phone two times. If Face ID is set, scan your face to approve purchase.

Measure screen time

With your mighty iPhone XS Max, Apple makes sure you can measure your screen time so that you are not making use of your phone more than you should. It's not that hard to find the screen time tracker, just go in the **Settings** and select **Screen Time** utility.

With screen time utility, you can track how much you are using your phone and also find out t what apps are using up your valuable time. This will enable you to be able to set limits.

Use portrait mode

Have you ever seen he wonders of the portrait mode in action before? It's just flat out beautiful. And with the iPhone XS Max, you can shoot in portrait mode with the front facing camera and the camera at the rear.

If you want to use portrait mode and witness it's abilities,

1. Open your camera app
2. Slide left on the menu slider. Stop when you see portrait
3. You should also see different lighting options like, Contour light, Natural light, Stage light. Choose lighting setup you wish
4. Hit shutter to take a picture. TO use to front camera, press the camera rotate symbol.

Using the depth control

Controlling the depth is a new option for the iPhones and sure the iPhone XS Max has it too. What depth control does is that, it enables you to control the blur that is the back ground of the in image even though you've already taken the photo.

To arm yourself with the depth control feature, just select the photo and you want to tweak, choose edit. The slider for depth control should show up now. Shift it to your heart's desire.

Create a Memoji

Apple's new iPhone XS Max allows you to create your Memoji without stress. In their previous phones, Apple released the Animoji and we were all thrilled. That came with the iPhone X.

But now what we have is Memoji. This Memoji enables user to make their own animated avatars. You can even control this avatar with your facial expressions.

To create a Memoji, all you have to do is
1. Open the **Message app** on your phone.
2. Click the **Appstore** symbol
3. Then the **small monkey** symbol
4. Select the **plus button** to **start**.

From here you can customize your face, hair color, skin and more. Once you're through with creating, hit **Done**

Turning Off Your Phone.

With the new iPhone XS Max, a task as simple as turning off the phone can be a real issue if you don't know what to do. Previously we all know that he button at the right side of the phone was the power button, but now since the side button is to launch Siri now, the question is, 'how I switch my phone off.

Piece of cake. Just press and hold the **volume down** or **up button** with the **side lock button** together at the same time. It should not take long before you see the option turn off your phone.

Switch On The True Tone Display

With the iPhone XS Max you have the true taste of the world's latest advancement in technology. And one of the improvements is the **True Tone**. This is the ability for your phone's screen to shift is color and temperature to adjust to the location you're in.

To enable **True Tone**, all you do is
1. Enter the **Settings**.
2. Choose **Display and Brightness**.
3. From here, toggle on **True Tone**

Using Memoji On FaceTime Calls

Memojis are fun use and can really spice up your conversations. With your iPhone XS Max, you can use both Memoji and Animoji in group calls or in one-on-one calls. You might be wondering how to do it?

1. Open the Face Time app on your phone. Start a call.
2. You should see a rectangular inlay that is at the bottom of the display, tap it
3. Select the Animoji symbol.
4. From here you have access to any Memoji that you've made and Animojis. Choose the one that you desire

Own Your Notifications

You know those entirely pointless notifications that make blaring noises and fill up your lock screen display? Yes those ones. You can have a lot more control over them now than before.

By control I mean you can quiet them down so that they go easy on your ears. Or so that they just go to the notification center peacefully. They don't have to appear on your lock screen, make noise and start to pop as a banner.

To be able to this;
1. Press and hold a notification as it comes and appears on the screen.
2. Select **Manage**
3. Choose **Deliver Quietly**.

Enable Display Zoom

Display zoom is a feature on the iPhone XS Max that makes whatever is on the screen of your phone to be a higher resolution. When this happens, the contents are a lot easier to read.

To switch on display zoom;
1. Enter **Settings**
2. Then **Brightness and View**
3. Choose **Display zoom.**
4. From here you can choose either **standard view** or **zoomed view.** There's a preview to show the differences between the two
5. Click on the one you desire. Your phone should restart for the resolution to change.

What **zoomed** does is that is shows you the same content but on a bigger display.

Enabling Do Not Disturb

Everyone wants themselves some quiet and peaceful time, free of disturbances. Maybe you're in your car and you want to avoid ringing from notifications or calls. You don't have to switch your phone off, all you do is turn on **Do Not Disturb**.

1. Enter **Settings**
2. Select **Do Not Disturb**.
3. Switch on the toggle beside **Do Not Disturb**

To state clearly who to accept calls from, select the **Allow Calls From** and specify your desired contact. With this option, you will only get calls from the people you wish.

Split The View

IPhone XS Max, the biggest iPhone in history. You have this extra screen space and it's just mindboggling to let all the extra screen space just go to waste. You can split the view of the phone to get extended view of apps

There are many apps that work with split view, certain websites too. Like the **New York Times**. With the **Mail app**, you get to see an extra preview screen along with your normal current view

To use the split view, you want to swipe down from the top right of the display and unlock the rotation lock sign. Now open an app. As long as the website or app is compatible with split screen, it should work.

Switch To One-Handed Mode

Since you've gotten your 6-inch iPhone XS Max, have you tried to navigate the screen and type messages using only one hand? If you have then you'll understand what I'm talking about. It can cause some serious hand ache.

But to relive the pain, Apple as provided the One-Handed mode that make the keyboard squeeze either to the right or to the left.

To enable One-Handed mode,
1. Go to **Settings**
2. Select **General**
3. Then **Keyboards**
4. Choose **One-Handed keyboard**

That will make it to be switched on all the time you want to type a message.

If you don't want it to be on always, you can just;
1. Go to iMessage.
2. When the keyboard is open, press and hold the emoji key that is on the left corner of

the screen and select either the right side or left side keyboard

3. To turn it off, press and hold the icon like before and chose middle keyboard

Rescue Your Home Button.

As must have noticed, the home button of the iPhone XS Max has been thrown out to the garbage. And for old users of iPhone who decided to get the iPhone XS Max for liberation, it can be a bit confusing to cope and learn all the gestures.

There's no problem, we just gather our army and get the home button back. Of course you now it's not the physical home button, we are getting a virtual one. Well at least it's something.

To enable the home button,

1. Fire up the **Settings app**
2. Enter **General**
3. Move to **Accessibility**
4. Select **Assistive touch**.

Chapter 4

How To Use Apple Pay

It is now ever easy to use Apple pay. It can even be done through the iMessage app. All you do to activate is place the top of your phone near the **NFC** card terminal while putting your finger on the iPhone's sensor for Touch ID. But to be able to perform all these wonders, you've got set Apple pay up first.

Setting Up The Apple Pay

1. Open **Wallet**
2. Select **Add Credit or Debit card**.
3. Put your card details. Your card will now be verified with your bank
4. Once that is done, you are able to use Apple Pay.

Using The Apple Pay.

1. Put your phone near the card reader and what will appear on the screen should be the image of your card.
2. If you use Touch ID, Place your finger on the Touch ID sensor. Once your fingerprint is confirmed, you're golden.

If you want another card, press the one that is on the screen and select a different card. Real simple, uh?

However if your phone uses Face ID like iPhone X and higher, the process is a little different. It's not hard though. You just click twice on the side button. Then put your face to the camera so it can scan your face. After this, you simply hold the phone toward the card reader. Double click the side button again, if you want to use another card and just select a different card.

Chapter 5

Tips for using iOS 12 effectively

Saving Your Passwords

In the iOS 12 there a totally cool feature that helps users be able to follow up on their passwords. The new iOS is armed with a feature called **AutoFill Passwords**. This is usually kept in the iCloud keychain.

With this, you can add your own username and passwords from your **Settings app** to set for only some apps and websites. This feature will fill in your information automatically for you once you use Face ID or Touch ID after it identifies the ones that are logged

Ability To Turn On 'Do Not Disturb' During Bedtime.

The **Do Not Disturb** option got totally revamped in the iOS 12. With its extra feature, you are able to customize it more to suit your taste. Not only can you state clearly what times you want **Do Not Disturb** to be on at day, you can even set it to Bedtime mode.

If you set it, this will quiet down all the notifications all the way till the morning. To let you know that it the feature is set, the screen will display just the date and time and become dim.

Measuring Objects With An App.

Using the camera of your iPhone, iOS 12 allows you to measure objects with AR. When you use the measure app, you'll be able to measure different objects.

All you do is,

1. Open the **Measure app**.
2. Fix your iPhone's camera on the object to measure
3. Follow the guides it gives to line up your phone correctly.
4. Next, to view the measurements, you just click the display

Every display will always show the option to switch form inches to centimeters. Of course it doesn't give an accurate measurement like a hardware tape rule, it is really handy if you just want to take a quick measurement of an item.

Insert Siri shortcuts

There's a new advancement with Siri in the iOS 12. It's the option to add immediate actions and shortcut to Siri. Thought this option is still in beta for now and you can't do plenty with it, there are still some perks you can enjoy.

Like how you can set a voice commands so that Siri can do some specific tasks. Example, **View New photos.**

If you want to set a voice command'

1. Enter your **Settings**.
2. Selects **Siri and Search**
3. Click **My Shortcuts**

Once that is open you will be able select anyone that Siri suggests.

Track your screen time

In the iOS 12, apple is trying to urge us to use our phones lesser so we can have time for other important activities. There's this new feature, **Screen time**.

Screen time is an opportunity for you to set Downtime, check your phone usage and find out which apps are really eating away your time. When you use down time, you are able to put away your phone by restraining some applications from forwarding notifications.

Place Limits on apps

This is also one of the perks of screen time. It enables you to set app limits. This will enable you to reduce the time you spend on certain apps. You will be able to set how long the ban should last and for which days.

If you want to set app limits.

1. Fire up the **Settings app**
2. Move to **Screen time**
3. Then **App limits**. Select the groups of apps you want to set limit. Click the **Add**

Easy Force Closing apps.

With the iOS 12, the process of force closing apps is a lot simpler. Not only simpler also quicker. All you do is swipe up from the bottom of the display and just start swiping the apps you want to quit like that.

Y'know, previously force closing apps on phones without home button on previous iOS will have to take a longer method. You'll have to swipe up and hold down and wait before a minus sign will appear, then you now click

But now with newer phones like the iPhone XS and XS Max, they all have the iOS 12, so the process is a lot simpler.

Chapter 6

How To Use Siri On Your Iphone

Siri is the ever helpful apple voice assistant that you dish out commands to on your iPhone and it just it just carries it out for you.

But something to note is that there's not a specific app icon for Siri that you just tap and it open. So how then do you access Siri. For newer generations of iPhones, accessing Siri can be a little confusing even if you have been using previous versions of iPhone. All of that we will cover here

How to invoke Siri

By Clicking the home button or side button
On older versions of iPhone, pressing and holing the home button on your device will call up Siri. But on the iPhone X and higher, you summon Siri by pressing the button at the side of the phone.

By using the Bluetooth headset button.

If you use a headset that has remote, press and hold the button at the center and you should hear a ding.

By saying hey Siri

If your iPhone is iOS 8 or higher, you can summon Siri hands free by saying 'Hey Siri'. But you've got to first set it up.

1. Got to **Settings**
2. Choose **Siri & Search**
3. Enable **Listen For** 'Hey Siri' and obey the prompts it provides
4. From now you can summon Siri without having to press anything just say **"Hey Siri"**

What Can Siri do for you,

- Send messages for you
- Set a timer for you
- Play music
- Send tweets
- Check the weather
- Schedule events
- Send emails

- Calculate
- Find locations

Here are some things you can ask Siri

- 'Hey Siri, Set an alarm for 6 am'
- 'Hey Siri, What is the time New York?'
- 'Hey Siri, schedule a meeting with Sarah for Tuesday at 11oclock
- 'Hey Siri, how cold will it be today?'
- 'Hey Siri, remind me to do the dishes?'
- 'Hey Siri, play me Roar by Katy Perry'
- 'Hey Siri, call David Randall'
- 'Hey Siri, open the Settings App'
- 'Hey Siri, how do I say hello in Spanish?'
- 'Hey Siri, who is the President of Iceland?'
- 'Hey Siri, turn off Bluetooth'

How to type and ask Siri

If you're the type that doesn't really fancy talking to Siri, you don't have to say something. You can just type your command. Though you'll have to set it up first

Here's how.

1. Enter **Settings**
2. Go to **General**
3. Select **Accessibility**
4. Move down to Siri and click the line
5. Switch on **Type To Siri**
6. The next time you activate Siri, all you do is type in your command

Tips To Ensure That Siri Serves You Well

While the apples virtual assistant is known for its top notch abilities, you may encounter some problems with it. Implement these few tips to allow Siri to better

Control how long Siri will listen

You have the power to control how long Siri will continue to encode your commands. You don't have to wait for it to recognize that you have stopped talking.

Just make sure that while you're asking your question or saying your command, you're holding down the power button

Alter Siri's language.

One of the key reasons why Siri may not understand your commands well can be because of your language. Even in English. Let's say you speak UK English. Siri may misinterpret your commands. So what you want to do is set the English to 'English (United Kingdom)

To adjust the language,
1. Enter the **Settings**
2. Go to **Siri and Search**
3. Select Language
4. Choose your desired language.

Having Smooth Data Connection

If you don't have data connection, Siri won't work. How Siri functions is that it records your voice and sends it to a server which converts your sayings and gives it back as text.

So if you're not connected to the internet, Siri is not going to work.

Changing Siri's gender

If you're a male and you prefer to have a male virtual brother around, you can switch the gender. Same goes for females.

Just,

1. Enter **Settings**
2. Then **Siri and Search**
3. Choose **Siri Voice**
4. Select your preferred voice.

Chapter 7

How To Maintain Your iPhone

We all know that iPhones are not biscuit change. They cost high. Well, they give superb quality so they are very well worth it. But such an investment will go to total waste if you don't take proper care of your treasure.

So here are some iOS maintenance tips for your consumption.

Put The Unwanted In The Garbage Truck

Do you remember that game that your buddy told you to try out and you felt it was total trash? Or yes, that app your neighbor introduced to you only for to find that it was a complete waste of time. Yes those applications. I'm pretty sure they are still sitting there in you app list

Throw them out and send them packing immediately. Not only do they use up the space of the phone, they also make it sluggish and your device slow. To delete an app, press and hold the app until it shakes like it's waving 'hey look at me' and delete or press the X at the corner.

Back Them Up

It's funny how many people do the bad stuff and only few do the good, like backing up your iPhones. You need to train yourself so that it becomes a habit.

Reason why backing up is so essential is because of this. Let's say your iPhone gets missing (I really hope that doesn't happen) or you there was a software update gone wrong or your device becomes faulty, retrieving your files will be almost impossible.

So don't wait for me, just back your phone up. You can back your phone up with iCloud or iTunes. In fact what's stopping you, just do both!

Update iOS

You be like 'Who needs an update. My iOS is just fine'. And I want you discard that feeling and throw it far away.

You need an update. With every new iOS there are fixes to bugs, updates for security, and brand new features and perks. You stick to your old iOS and it will be like you're living in the Stone Age.

What more, updating is like the easiest thing to do. Since we have OTA (Over The Air), updating iOS is just a matter of minutes.

To update,
1. Make sure to back up your phone as we warned earlier
2. Enter **Settings**
3. Then **General**
4. Then Choose **Software update**.
5. If an update is available, click **Download and install**.

Phone case and Screen protector

We all know how phone cases and screen protectors saves our lives every once in a while. Okay, not our life per say, it's our phones. Whenever your phone drops, a protective phone case will help to absorb the effect and shock of the fall.

And screens, oh screens are really special. And believe me when I say that you do not want them to break. So just buy a screen protector.

When you're purchasing either of the two, make sure it's of good quality and the design is what you desire.

Chapter 8

Prolonging Your iPhones Battery Life.

As with maintenance of phones, we all know how much battery means to us. Check out these tips to extend your phones battery life.

Forget Quitting Apps

You may probably be doing this, quitting apps regularly, I usually do so too in the past. But stop. you might think that you're saving you're battery, but actually you're degrading it.

In 2014, Apple explained to us that quitting apps sucks more battery as the next time you want to open the app, it will start all over again thereby, eating the batter.

Using The Auto Brightness Option.

Using full screen brightness sucks away your battery and I'm sure you know that. Unless you really need the extra brightness, don't be stubborn just use auto brightness.

This adjusts the screens brightness to the surroundings you're in.

Turn Low Power Mode On

Normally when you're phone reaches 20%, you'll be prompted to switch to low power mode. But you don't have to wait for your phone to urge you before you switch it. You can do it right after you finishing charging.

Low power mode stops all the background tasks and gives you more battery.

Turn Off Bluetooth.

It's not a new thing that putting your Bluetooth on regularly reduces the battery life. So if you're not using the Bluetooth, just put it off

Disclaimer

In as much as the author believes beginners will find this book helpful in learning how to use the iPhone XS Max, it is only a small book. It should not be relied upon solely for all iPhone tricks and troubleshooting.

About the author

Stephen Rock has been a certified apps developer and tech researcher for more than 12 years. Some of his 'how to' guides have appeared in a handful of international journals and tech blogs. He loves rabbits.

Facebook page @ Techgist